We Who Dream

poems by

Gwynn O'Gara

Finishing Line Press
Georgetown, Kentucky

We Who Dream

Copyright © 2023 by Gwynn O'Gara
ISBN 979-8-88838-082-6 First Edition

All rights reserved under International and Pan-American Copyright Conventions. No part of this book may be reproduced in any manner whatsoever without written permission from the publisher, except in the case of brief quotations embodied in critical articles and reviews.

ACKNOWLEDGMENTS

My heartfelt gratitude to these journals, anthologies, and presses for publishing my work:

Marsh Hawk Review: "Summer Sung"
Oyez Review: "Just This"
Paddlefish: "Miracles October 2004"
Santa Fe Literary Review: "The Artichoke Sutra"
Spoon River Literary Review: "The House of Masks"
Syracuse Cultural Workers Women's Art Calendar: "Rhythm"
The Comstock Review: "God's Mouth"
The Evansville Review: "The Spirits That Lend Strength Are Invisible"
Fog and Light, San Francisco through the Eyes of the Poets Who Live Here, Blue Light Press: "Magic From Chinatown"
Sisters Born, Sisters Found Anthology, A Diversity of Voices on Sisterhood, Wordforest Press: "Paper Cranes"
World of Change Anthology, New Way Media Fest: "Poetry Teacher"
Snake Woman Poems, Beatitude Press, 1983: "We Can't Get Out of Here, We Own the Place"

The epigraph from Frida Kahlo is from *Pocket Frida Kahlo Wisdom,* hardie grant books

Publisher: Leah Huete de Maines
Editor: Christen Kincaid
Cover Art: Mark Casey Milestone
Author Photo: Rob Catterton
Cover Design: Elizabeth Maines McCleavy

Order online: www.finishinglinepress.com
also available on amazon.com

Author inquiries and mail orders:
Finishing Line Press
PO Box 1626
Georgetown, Kentucky 40324
USA

Table of Contents

Song for a Bride 1

Cloud Heaven 2

We Can't Get Out of Here, We Own the Place 3

Another Way 4

Love Crazed 5

Lyric From Mall #116,001 6

The Pharaoh's Daughter 7

Magic from Chinatown 8

Thresholds Are for Crossing 9

The Audacity of Rest 10

The House of Masks 11

The Roads of Sleep 12

The Tent Door Closes and Opens 13

We Who Dream 14

Poetry Teacher 15

God's Mouth 16

Miracles October 2004 17

Paper Cranes 19

Just This 20

Rhythm 21

The Artichoke Sutra 22

Spider Housewife 23

Safe Home 24

Summer Sung 25

The Spirits That Lend Strength Are Invisible 26

*Deep thanks to friends, family and fellow poets, including
Rob Catterton, Chris Catterton,
Greg O'Gara, Nancy Dafoe, Gail Onion and Nancy Dougherty.*

Song for a Bride

There is nothing like it

Beloved, a good man purring at your breast
the cellar full of groats and salt
your future brewing like soup on the stove

You learn about proportion
and the language your lover dreams in

Exploring the landscape you will age in
you send your boats out, low in the water
with the bulk of your history
quick and shimmery with delight

Sometimes his boats come to you so weighted down
you go on strike until he unloads them himself
or your heart cracks enough to let him in

Sometimes on unmarked anniversaries
of the first time you understood each other
or his first appearance in your dreams
your boats sail off together
no longer servants but envoys
meeting and going off on their own

Cloud Heaven

Bed of horny mornings and hard-ons
mountains of pillows
and rules to break.

Egos entwined at our feet
I dream the first night.
Our souls look down and laugh.

You fondle one breast
press behind me in the dark.
Last mouth at night.

Crumpled morning glimpses.
Our first home.
A baby would fit right in.

We Can't Get Out of Here, We Own the Place

I kneel before you like a beaver
dance around you like a hummingbird.
My cells splash again.
A heron takes root in my neck
a cellar full of oats appears
in every house in the neighborhood.
Wild dream come to rest in my arms
sister in man's flesh
wink of nature
amorous as the dawn.

Another Way

Croon through the mall 'til shoppers find
what they want isn't there but back home
or buried under leaves or at sea.
Sing green shoots cracking the pavement.
Croak your desire under water and stars.
Bless hope with glad work.
Pray to and for the bees
leaving them asleep in the petals.
Name babies for muses and trees.
Undress lovers down to their vowels.

Love Crazed

When you brought me strawberries
dripping wild red, I knew
you and I were perfectly matched.

I like pretty things. It's not a weakness,
a woman's sport or part of my *knafs*. It's my gift
to notice tiles and towels perfectly match.

Thumbelina in her tulip petal boat can't
go live in the mud with Toad's son. Like my mom
and step-dad, they're the opposite of perfectly matched.

Freakishly strong roots reads the Supertunia label.
Sometimes we grow roots around stones or air.
We and certain petunias are perfectly matched.

Bears chase salmon into the shallows, then grab them.
They miss a lot yet one bear ate 42 salmon in a day.
She and the river were perfectly matched.

You think I laugh too much? Last time I was with
you, all I did was cry. Such differences reveal
you and I are mysteriously yet perfectly matched.

Gwynn, you always were a fool about men. Ask him
to send you an apricot from his wedding feast.
You'll taste how he and she are perfectly matched.

Lyric from Mall #116,001

Oh, round meat man in the grocery store
    roll with me in the back behind
        boxes of canned apple juice.

Oh, whiskery contractor in the parking lot
    lay me down in the dark of your truck
        beside your dogs and tools.

Oh, glowing guy in the vitamin store
    help me pop E's and C's and come
        in monumental bursts of supplemental bliss.

Oh, studious fellow eyeing the frozen dinners
    bend me over the deepfreeze
        'til the ice cream turns to soup.

I'll think of you when
    longing needs a different face
        across the kitchen table.

The Pharaoh's Daughter

I don't care what you do with my body.
Wrap me in twine, pluck my eyes and heart
and plunge them into patient strangers.
Let that fat scribe write anything.
Lies, endearments, praise
they're all the same on a windy day.

Carry my ashes to our favorite spot
and order me a cabernet
or leave them at home collecting dust on the mantel.
Just make sure I've got an alabaster jug like Dad's.
Oblivion and gin fill his but leave mine empty.

Let my spirit pour like oil
and slip through the gods' fingers
to return to a bed of rock
my only companion a turtle
my only weakness love.

Magic From Chinatown

Daddy's treat in a plastic bag
black-gray clam
smaller than a quarter
we submerged in the kitchen sink.

Hour by hour
the bivalve soaked up water
then suddenly cracked open.
In another hour
a stem emerged
and over the next few hours
lengthened toward our faces.

Eventually
pink and yellow petals unfurled.

Every secret, stranger, lover, moon
a surprise
staggering up through watery depths
toward light
prying itself open from within
blossoming.

Flower Face, I call you,
Camellia Ears,
Rose Lips.

Thresholds Are for Crossing

Bowing
        you enter the sea.
                Looking up the winding stairs
                      you take the first step.
              Coaxing the horse
        you rub her neck.
At the river's mouth
              the island washes away.

The Audacity of Rest

After mating for months in the sharky sea, harbor seals
haul up at the river's mouth and heave themselves
into hammocks of sand, dreaming of endless eels.

Docents with binoculars patrol the sand, protecting them
from us, daffy public out for exercise and adventure, halted by
a snoring monument to laze and loll, a slow circus of siestas.

Sleeping beauties full of octopus and squid, you are awake
and we are dreaming. Teach us to keep a safe distance
and drowse against each other as today sprints by.

The House of Masks

Waves thudder like lead coins on cobbles.
An anchor of rebar washes ashore.
Scolding next door. Tears. The rose laughs.
The octopus fledges among rocks.
The braided girl kneels, her arms around
a hundred callas. Did Diego paint the lilies'
hollow stalks dense as pumpkin stems
to salute the work of harvest, restoring
the heart beside the knife in the hand?
Feathers nudge the air. Egrets jab the tide.
Heron collects questions for the night.
Would you rather be a guest slipping
through the world, or alone clinging to a rock?

The Roads of Sleep

The nurse gives them shoes for their children.
No one else sweetens the wages they live on
but the women tending aloe and roses.

Lucky ones find old hives buried by their fathers.
Their uncles drew maps to the trees
and their mothers sang them along the roads of sleep.

Others dream of mercy, the music of home
and the tired voice of the nurse,
Take these. They're for you.

Goat stink wafts past fence posts in fields
where they bend. Praying in their letters,
Pay the grocer. I will find my way home.

The Tent Door Opens and Closes

Bees drown in lap pools. Racket of jungle birds. In the cove
La Sirena soaks. Flounder brushes a knee. Divers clank
machetes, harvesting stars. The black dog with yellow
eyes slips the leash. Smelling of sweat and lime, the dark
vine of a man washes me with pomegranate and aloe.
All night we dawn with lascivious cries.

We Who Dream
> *"my cells, which are my stars . . ."* Frida Kahlo

Haloed by redwoods, a vulture sky
and plump, comical geese,
the soul-body of Guadalupe shimmers.

North on our backs, around our necks,
in our skin, snuggled in suitcases,
constant in cages, flowing underground.

September's feathered heat and
bountiful barbeques. Tunneling cold tickles
our legs through the water's massage.

Girls and boys play-fight for swan, burger
and unicorn floats. Reborn in dream-water,
lovers cradle one another. Kids scream.

Late afternoons a breeze from the Pacific.
Geese gabble in, splash down with cartoon faces.
Without wings we made it. Lost a few. Lost a lot.

Among thorns children, friends, work,
hoodies unzipped with sweat and song,
we who dream know there are no borders.

Poetry Teacher

You want to say—
don't worry about being fat
what gives you the greatest joy?
don't get into the car when your mother's drunk
go easy with the weed
don't let fear of imagined reactions stop you
sometimes you have to be the parent
god, I hope you're using birth control
your attitude sucks
you're going to break down and smash something,
probably yourself
your loneliness frightens me
don't join the military just yet
I'm sorry your mother died
I'm sorry your father doesn't talk with you
just wait, someday someone will understand you
how many people did it take to make you this angry?
who told you you were garbage?—
but what you say is
Keep writing

God's Mouth

> It's beautiful when a whale blows his nose in the air.
> Through a crack in Mismaloya's seawall an
> iguana's sussing eyeball. Four yellow
> butterflies in a gale.
> Torso-boulders stripped
> by earthquake,
> pelican eyes wise with food.
> Sand scrapes blood from
> a boy's thigh.
> The rich keep trying to lock
> the beach.
> Nellie captains her own boat,
> *I'm strong inside, too.*
> Up the canyon women wash clothes
> in the laughing river.
> Children shriek,
> frigate birds loom.
> Octopus fields,
> shrimp beds, a wealth of sewage.
> *Love*, God roars, their breath stinky, salty, sweet. *Love.*

Miracles October 2004

Game 4 of the Series, Boston's up by three in the 6th
my brother's in Shock/Trauma hooked up to a breathing machine

the moon's almost fully eclipsed
at the B&B I'm eating ice cream sweet as Lowe's slider

a fellow guest heads a little investment club in Virginia
starts chatting

the Sox haven't won in 83 years
the breathy whine goes on about day trading, his dust of 9/11

Arroyo relieves Lowe in the 7th, the Cards get two men on base
at a commercial I dash outside to catch the disappearing moon

paunchy, bearded like players on the field
he opines the loss of moral values

dismisses cities, the eastern seaboard
and by inference, any race but his

I check the moon, its clean light deeper in shadow
the Sox put Embree in, Cards load the bases

his favorite stocks are Taser and Mace
I turn to look him in the eyes and miss the key play

outside, the light like water gone
Embree strikes out Luna in the 8th

the simple syrup voice drones on
the Sox don't score nor do the Cards

as a minister he saw miracles like pancreatic cancer disappear
I mention my brother

he tries to make nice but it involves more talking
I stop listening, give myself fully to the pleasure of the game

bottom of the 9th the moon passes out of shadow
Foulke comes in and wins it

the guy shuts up
the nurse adjusts the morphine drip

Paper Cranes

Every day since her sister died
the woman folds paper into birds.
Dozens of cranes dangle from beam,
molding, and mantel, crowding
her house with her sister's absence
and prayers for safe passage.

While she folds, the woman sees her sister
abandon a ragged tent beside a glacier
and ascend into the fiery dark.
She remembers bubbles in the tub,
Chinese pajamas for Christmas,
pleasure in her sister's pliable nature.

She lost count of the birds.
She feels her way along folds
she no longer needs to see,
pushes needle and thread through
each bird's heart and tethers it:
her fingers know the knots.

One day the needle breaks.
She means to get a new one
but life claims her back—son,
husband, work, the comfrey
in the side yard that just won't die.
Arriving home one evening

the cranes annoy her.
She doesn't need reminding:
grief has settled in her bones.
She yanks one down, the pin
flies out of sight. She'll call a friend,
take them all down tonight.

Just This

I clean off the dust of a hard winter
and find a new lamp for my desk.

Bowing, I set out seeds and bulbs.
Roots and worms slip through my fingers.

I breathe the wind of the future.
If only now were over.

Where does this distress come from?
Was it born when others ruled my life?

Or when I lost them? Will it make me
a better woman, more awake to the present?

Let me find something to give you, friend.
Perhaps this emptiness would be of use.

Rhythm

Late afternoon the dog comes to my study
and rubs her softness against me.
Now, say her eyes.
Even the patient know urgency,
the dreamy wake to appetite.
Among the trees she greets old friends,
exults in the warmth of a new hand.
At home I fill her bowl.

So the heart finds where we hide
among strangers or preoccupations
and tells us it is time.

Feed what is hungry.
Air what is stale.
Pick up pen or phone
and pronounce the words
practiced so long in silence.

Or lie down in the sun with the grass.
Neither bless nor curse,
simply change.

The Artichoke Sutra

The Kelp Mothers steer her along milky roads
to the bright region inside the fog.

Coastal lotuses with stalks like oak saplings
shimmer in rows to the sea.

Wild when time was counted in moons
owl-eyed food of goddess and surfer.

Glaucous sunflower of stubborn love,
cleansing thistle of longevity.

Chakra of arms and hands
our first shield also lifts and bears.

Bountiful as the muscles ringing our shoulders
spine-tipped bracts open.

With fervent teeth we scrape the meat,
shave the choke to the flower bud we eat.

My cousin cups a globe in her hands.
Scrumptious heart. Core of the song.

Remembering her sister, she offers it to me.
Blood and oil attend. Food of the blossom.

Hub of the blessing. Such loss in flesh
as well as sea, such silence in each song.

Teach us how to bear.
Feed us as we mourn.

Spider Housewife

On the lookout for a baby and fresh news,
his father in the hospital, my daily
temperature. Balls of hair line the hall,
webs tax the corners.

Piles of bills and dishes,
sheets smelling of poppies.
You wrestle the night in each other,
blossom no one sees inside.

Safe Home

I lift a foot to smash a snail
                        and remember.
I fold a leaf to squoosh a slug
                        and remember.
I tug a weed and feel
                        its roots tug back.
All day I stop and remember . . .

Summer Sung

Grotto with hummingbirds, tea and nutmeg,
nectarines spilling the meaning of life.
Enough! chant orange buckwheat and fuchsia.
E*nough!* the swaying trees keen for brothers.

Infinite gardening, dilapidated joy,
making art not war.
Strange folk snag the big world.
Without golf, sex or big bucks
how will they lend me an ear?

The soul's midriff plays in the sun.
Her ample shoulders shade me in a spring-rooted lake.
Baseballs rise and set.
The home-run moon fills our bags with popcorn and relief.
Hooray for the fence lizard who evades the crow's beak.

The Spirits That Lend Strength Are Invisible
From the Navajo

The grandmothers came to me on the wind
the furious wind from the west they came
from the sun as I rocked and rocked
beneath the sky the sky of one color
pale as my baby's skin and as bright

I saw them and heard them as I rocked
and rocked for dear life coming out of me
coming down slowly out of me as I rocked
back and forth back and forth as he pushed
out of and back into me out of and back into me

The grandmothers came to me and whispered
Breathe Rock Wait Open
they came with the wind out of the sun
they came from their cave hidden in time
from their procession down to the sea
where they prepared me years before in dreams

They came and brought strength and peace so I
could rock into the dusk and on into the darkness
rocking and breathing and fighting the peaceful way
to let my baby deliver himself to me from his cave
their cave that is endless and built of moons

I rocked and I rocked and the grandmothers
came to me and whispered their words of power
to help me through the long disengagement of my son
on wheelchairs cornstalks mops and meteorites
they traveled and turned through the white sky

They gathered around my head in whorls of cooling
fire and they gave me water from the sun that
burned me cool and they took from me my
separateness—no longer—not ever—would I be
sola and they eased me open to let out my son

So I rocked forward to become a mother
and backward to join them the ancient ones
holders of life bringers of life

Gwynn O'Gara is a West Coast poet and writer inspired by the natural world. She loves to be outside, exploring, tending, and listening.

Daughter of a newspaper man and a NYC ad copywriter, O'Gara grew up in a home where clear, truthful language was venerated. As an adolescent living in Mexico City, Gwynn first experienced the world's different colors, music, and possibilities.

Reading and performing in San Francisco's North Beach, Gwynn came into her own, forging friendships with Beat poet Bob Kaufman and jazz poet David Moe. She and Kaufman met at a poetry festival when they started reciting Eliot together. Her book *Snake Woman Poems* was published in 1983 with an introduction by Nanos Valoritis.

O'Gara served as Poet Laureate of Sonoma County from 2010-2011. While a California Poet in the Schools, she guided students of all backgrounds and ages to express themselves through poetry, song and recitation. Gwynn continues her celebration with readings and reciting.

Gwynn is grateful to her family and friends, and her teachers Sebastian Balfour, William Rosenfeld and Denise Levertov. She lives with pianist Rob Catterton north of San Francisco among fruit trees, oaks, and redwoods.

Published in *Spoon River Literary Review, The Evansville Review,* and *descant,* her poetry has also appeared in the anthologies *Know Me Here*, a collection of women's voices, and *Lost Orchard*. Her full-length book, *Snake Woman Poems*, was followed by the chapbooks *Fixer-Upper, Winter at Green Haven,* and *Sea Cradles.*

www.ingramcontent.com/pod-product-compliance
Lightning Source LLC
Chambersburg PA
CBHW022127090426
42743CB00008B/1035